The Future of TECHNOLOGY

What Is the Future of Self-Driving Cars?

ReferencePoint Press®

San Diego, CA

Other books in The Future of Technology series

The Future of
TECHNOLOGY

What Is the Future of Self-Driving Cars?

Stephanie Watson

ReferencePoint Press®

San Diego, CA

For more information, contact:
ReferencePoint Press, Inc.
PO Box 27779
San Diego, CA 92198
www.ReferencePointPress.com

LIBRARY OF CONGRESS CATALOGING-IN-PUBLICATION DATA

Name: Watson, Stephanie, author.
Title: What is the future of self-driving cars? / by Stephanie Watson.
Description: San Diego, CA : ReferencePoint Press, Inc., [2017] | Series: The future of technology series | Audience: Grade 9 to 12. | Includes bibliographical references and index.
Identifiers: LCCN 2016004755 (print) | LCCN 2016013276 (ebook) | ISBN 9781682820643 (hardback) | ISBN 9781682820650 (eBook)
Subjects: LCSH: Autonomous vehicles--Juvenile literature. | Automobiles--Automatic control--Juvenile literature.
Classification: LCC TL152.8 .W38 2017 (print) | LCC TL152.8 (ebook) | DDC 629.222--dc23
LC record available at http://lccn.loc.gov/2016004755

Contents

Important Events in the Development of Self-Driving Cars

1939
At the World's Fair in New York, General Motors presents a model of a futuristic 1960 city, complete with self-driving cars.

1979
Hans Moravec at the Stanford University Artificial Intelligence Laboratory uses a computer to make a cart (the Stanford Cart) travel across a room on its own.

1995
A self-driving Pontiac minivan created by Carnegie Mellon researchers travels from Washington, DC, to San Diego, California.

1977
Japanese engineer Sadayuki Tsugawa builds an intelligent car with a computer that allows it to ride along a rail without a driver.

1940   1950   1960   1970   1980   1990

1956
A General Motors promotional film portrays a family speeding along a track highway in a self-driving car.

1986
German engineer Ernst Dickmanns tests a self-driving van guided by cameras and sensors.

1991
Dean Pomerleau, a roboticist at Carnegie Mellon University, modifies a Chevy van with a video camera and laser range finder; using a computer, Pomerleau "teaches" the van to drive.

1995
A Mercedes-Benz that Dickmanns equips with cameras, sensors, and microprocessors drives nearly 1,000 miles (1,609 km) from Munich, Germany, to Copenhagen, Denmark, without a human steering or operating the gas.

2004
The Defense Advanced Research Projects Agency (DARPA) holds its first Grand Challenge in California's Mojave Desert; its goal is to develop autonomous vehicles for military use.

2005
DARPA holds its second Grand Challenge.

2010
Google reports that its self-driving cars have traveled more than 140,000 miles (225,308 km).

2008
Google launches its self-driving car project.

2016
Secretary of Transportation Anthony Foxx announces he is giving the Department of Transportation six months to draft national guidelines governing the way self-driving cars are tested and regulated; President Barack Obama pledges nearly $4 billion for the research and testing of self-driving car technology.

2005 **2010** **2015**

2007
DARPA's first Urban Challenge is held in a simulated urban street environment at the former George Air Force Base in Victorville, California.

2011
Nevada passes a law allowing self-driving cars on its roads, becoming the first state to pass such a law.

2014
Audi releases its traffic jam assistant, a semiautonomous feature that allows a car to stay in its lane in highway traffic.

2009
Google's fleet of self-driving Toyota Priuses begin making test-drives around the San Francisco area.

2015
Tesla releases an autopilot feature for its S and X models.

Introduction

The Driverless Car

From Theory to Application

Self-driving cars, also known as autonomous cars, driverless cars, or robot cars, are vehicles that can steer, brake, and carry passengers from one place to another—all without human intervention. To drive themselves, cars must use a combination of technologies. Sensors such as video cameras, light detection and ranging, and radar capture information about the car's position relative to objects around it. They help the car stay within its lane, detect traffic lights and stop signs, and avoid other vehicles and pedestrians. Global positioning system (GPS) software provides a map that helps the car travel along its route and reach its destination. A computer in the car's trunk gathers all the information from these sensors and sends directions to operate the steering wheel, gas, and brakes. A set of instructions or rules, called algorithms, help the car make decisions in much the same way a human driver would.

In Las Vegas, Nevada, a gray Audi A7 pulls into the entrance of the Mandarin Oriental hotel parking garage, stops, and turns off. A woman steps out of the car. She pulls out her smartphone and touches a box on the screen marked *Park*. Inside the car, the dashboard controls light up. A monitor pops up from the dash. As the woman turns to leave the garage, the car's ignition turns back on. The Audi drives into the garage with no one in the driver's seat, its steering wheel turning as if by some unseen force. The car navigates its way to an open spot in the garage and backs in perfectly. Then the car turns itself off. When the woman returns to the parking garage a short time later, she presses *Pickup* on her cell phone. The car's lights pop on, and the engine roars back to life. The Audi pulls out of the spot and drives itself back to where the woman is waiting at the garage entrance.

What appeared to be a magic trick—a car parking itself in a garage—was actually the display of a very real technology. Audi was showcasing its new autonomous parking system, called Piloted Parking, for visitors to the 2013 Consumer Electronics Show. The so-called magic behind this self-parking marvel were sensors Audi had placed around the car. These sensors helped the car find its way around the garage and find an open space. Wi-Fi and lasers in the garage helped the car navigate. A computer in the car gathered the information its sensors received and quickly analyzed them to make driving decisions like a human driver. The computer gave directions to operate the steering wheel, gas pedal, brakes, and shifting and get the car where it needed to go—no human needed. After seeing Audi's self-parking feature in action, a *Car and Driver* magazine reporter called it "nothing short of astounding."[1]

The Future of Today

Cars that drive themselves might seem like an idea straight out of a science fiction movie. Yet the technology needed for cars to steer through traffic, avoid other vehicles and pedestrians, and carry passengers safely to their destinations is here, and it has been developing for decades. The first ideas for self-driving cars were hatched in the early part of the twentieth century. These visions of autonomous cars relied more on the road they drove on than on the cars themselves. Imaginative engineers of the 1930s proposed cars that could ride driverless down a track-like road, guided to their destination by radio signals from a control tower.

As computer technology improved, scientists were able to equip cars with sensors that allowed the vehicles to identify their surroundings and avoid any obstacles. The real push forward in self-driving car technology came at the turn of the twenty-first century, when a government agency challenged engineers to create a car that could operate entirely without human intervention.

With the right technology in place, several car companies and one computer technology company vied to be the first to put a self-driving car on the road. Each approached the challenge in a different way. Car companies like Audi, General Motors (GM), and Mercedes-Benz outfitted their existing cars with sensors and computers. Google engineered its car in reverse—shaping an automobile around a computer. As these companies now compete for supremacy in this new field, the winner could decide the fate of autonomous driving technology. The companies that are most successful in the market will determine whether autonomous cars are computers with wheels or cars outfitted with high-tech sensing and computing equipment.

WORDS IN CONTEXT

autonomous
Operating on its own; such as a car driving without a human at the wheel.

Like most infant technologies, autonomous cars have progressed with baby steps. Over a period of many years, companies have added self-driving features such as lane assist, collision warning, and self-braking. By 2015 a few cars were able to drive without a human hand on the wheel or foot on the brake, but only in certain situations, such as in slow traffic.

Self-Driving Cars of the Twenty-First Century

Experts predict that fully self-driving cars could become a reality by the middle of the twenty-first century. Some analysts say these cars could revolutionize the way people get from place to place. For one thing, the computers that operate self-driving cars never fall asleep or get distracted. They are less likely than a human driver to misjudge a turn or fail to see a car in the rearview mirror. The kind of precision this technology offers could reduce or

Traffic congestion on highways and surface streets is a problem for both drivers and communities. Driverless automobiles used as shuttle services for multiple commuters may reduce the number of cars on the road and ease gridlock and pollution.

even prevent human error behind the wheel, which is the cause of most accidents. Fewer or no accidents could prevent expensive damage to cars and potentially save lives.

Driverless cars also have the potential to cut down on the number of vehicles on the road. Instead of owning a car, people could simply buy into an on-demand pickup service—like today's Uber or Lyft—but without a human driver at the wheel. Fewer cars on the roads would require less vehicle production and would produce less pollution. People who have not been able to drive because they are blind, disabled, or elderly could feel the freedom of traveling wherever they want to go without having to ask for a ride from a friend or relative. And autonomous cars could free up time, allowing people to catch up on work or read while on the road.

As promising as self-driving cars might be, the technology does have its risks. Computers and sensors don't fall asleep at the wheel, but they can still fail. Sometimes equipment breaks and computers crash. Computers can also fall prey to hacking, an issue computer companies have struggled with for many years. The price of the technology needed to produce driverless cars is still very high. Costs must come down enough to make these vehicles affordable to the masses.

Legal challenges also exist. States must pass laws to allow self-driving cars on their roads. Traffic laws may need to change to accommodate cars without human drivers. And the federal government must ensure that driverless cars operate the same way in every state.

A likely drop in accidents will affect the insurance industry too. When accidents do occur, a decision will need to be made about who is responsible—the carmaker, technology manufacturer, or the person who is in the car at the time? A vast reduction in accidents might even make insurance policies obsolete, changing the industry dramatically. Finally, for self-driving cars to be successful, consumers must be willing to entrust their lives and turn over control to a car, something current surveys show they are not quite ready to do.

Chapter 1

The Earliest Attempts at Self-Driving Cars

When the World's Fair opened in Flushing Meadows, New York, on April 30, 1939, it promised visitors a glimpse into the future. Themed "Building the World of Tomorrow," the fair offered a vision of hope and prosperity through technology at a time when Americans were just starting to recover from the financial turmoil of the Great Depression. The 44 million visitors who came to the fair witnessed futuristic exhibits, including an 8-foot-tall (2.4 m) robot named Elektro who walked, talked, and smoked a cigarette.

In the Futurama exhibit sponsored by car company GM, people waited in line for hours to see a miniature model of a 1960 city. Created by industrial designer Norman Bel Geddes, this city of the future envisioned towering skyscrapers topped with helicopter landing pads. Driverless cars sped along superhighways—operated by radio signals from a central control tower. Bel Geddes predicted, "These cars of 1960 and the highways on which they drive will have in them devices which will correct the faults of human beings as drivers. They will prevent the driver from committing errors."[2]

GM took its vision one step further in a 1956 promotional film in which a family time travels to 1976 in their 1950s Firebird. Once in the future, their automobile transforms into a turbine-powered jet car with a clear bubble roof. As the futuristic Firebird speeds along a track highway, the father speaks over the car's radio to a controller in a tower. When he tells the controller they are "all set for auto-control," the controller directs him to move to the track's center lane, which is equipped with an electrical control

Leonardo da Vinci's Vision

Cars weren't invented until the late nineteenth century, and self-driving cars are only recently coming to fruition. Yet more than five hundred years ago Italian artist Leonardo da Vinci sketched plans for a self-propelled vehicle.

Da Vinci was no stranger to invention. During his lifetime he envisioned flying machines, armored cars, parachutes, and cannons. In around 1478 he sketched a car that measured 5.5 feet (1.6 m) long and nearly 5 feet (1.5 m) wide. Like a wind-up toy, it had springs that were wound up by rotating the tires in the opposite direction. Once the brake was released, the car could travel about 130 feet (40 m) on its own. Wooden blocks between the gears gave the car programmable steering.

Curious about whether da Vinci's car could actually drive on its own, in 2004 engineers in Florence, Italy, began building a smaller-scale model. It took them four months, but at the end they concluded the design worked. "It was—or is—the world's first self-propelled vehicle," says Paolo Galluzzi, director of the Institute and Museum of the History of Science in Florence, who led the project.

Quoted in John Hooper, "Leonardo's Car Brought to Life," *Guardian*, April 24, 2004. www.theguardian.com.

strip. A receiver mounted on the front end of the car picks up a radio signal, which steers the car down the track. The family sits back and relaxes while the car drives them safely to their destination.

The film and World's Fair display weren't just fantasies. GM did try to make its Futurama vision a reality. It partnered with RCA (the Radio Corporation of America) to develop cars controlled by radio signals. These cars of the future were supposed to debut in the 1970s, but they never made it to market. "The stumbling block is you would need to retrofit all the freeways. There was actually a big effort to do that, a lot of funding went into it, a lot of studies but it never hit critical mass,"[3] explains Marc Weber, founding curator of the Internet History Program at the Computer History Museum.

GM's early vision of driverless automobiles relied more on redesigned roads than on new technology for cars. Yet the goals behind the project were the same as those of today's self-driving cars—to take the burden of driving off humans while improving safety on the roads.

Building the Technology

In the 1960s research shifted from a road-directed car to a self-directed one. For that to happen, cars would need to be equipped with sensors to scan the environment around them and with artificial intelligence to make decisions about their every move.

Sensors are a type of detector that measure a physical property—for example, light, heat, or movement. They then turn that measurement into a signal. College professor Warren Johnson developed one of the earliest sensors—the electric thermostat—in 1883. His invention was the predecessor to today's home thermostats, which use sensors to detect temperature and then trigger the heat to turn on or off as the temperature drops or rises. In cars, sensors detect the level of fuel in the gas tank and the temperature inside the engine.

Infrared sensors have been around since the 1940s. These sensors detect a type of heat radiation, which most objects give off. In doing so, the sensor can identify how far away one object is from another. In a car, an infrared sensor can identify obstacles like fallen tree branches or people in the road and determine the distance between one car and another to avoid a fender bender.

Artificial intelligence is the idea that computers can be taught to think, communicate, and make decisions independently, just as humans can. The term was first coined in the 1950s, the same decade in which English mathematician Alan Turing published his famous test for determining whether computers can think: the Turing test. A computer would pass the test if its communications were so intelligent that a human judge couldn't tell the difference between its responses and those of a real human being.

Self-Propelled Cart

Early computers were far too slow and cumbersome to pass for human. In the 1950s and 1960s, innovations in both hardware and computing languages made computers faster than ever before, able to process millions of operations per second. Yet they were still slow by today's standards. And they were massive, filling entire rooms. Their size made them impractical for use in a car.

For a vehicle at the time to use a computer to navigate, the computer would need to be close by, which wouldn't work with a moving car. But it could work in the confined setting of a laboratory. In the 1970s Hans Moravec at the Stanford University Artificial Intelligence Laboratory mounted a camera on a remote-controlled cart. Through a long cable, the camera sent images of the cart's surroundings to a mainframe computer. The computer then processed those images and used them to help the cart decide where to move. The Stanford Cart, as it was named, was the first robotic vehicle able to navigate obstacles without human help. It wasn't quick, though. The computer processing speed was so slow that the cart could travel only 3 feet (1 m) every ten to fifteen minutes. It took five hours to cross a room. Still, it was a start.

The GM Firebird II was a 1950s concept car built to allow drivers to relinquish control to an autopilot system using radio signals to guide the vehicle along a special highway track. The cost of retrofitting all the nation's highways, however, kept this car from ever reaching the market.

Artificial Intelligence and Self-Driving Cars

For a car to operate without a human behind the wheel, it needs artificial intelligence. In other words, a computer driver has to learn how to identify the environment around it and react to that environment as quickly and efficiently as a human brain. The computer needs to scan the road, identify the positions of other cars and pedestrians, and avoid any possible obstacles.

In 1949 British mathematician Alan Turing had predicted a future in which computers could do anything humans could. "I do not see why [the computer] should not enter any one of the fields normally covered by the human intellect, and eventually compete on human terms," he wrote in the *London Times*.

Yet the technology lagged behind its promise. When engineers began developing self-driving cars in the 1950s and 1960s, artificial intelligence was still very new. The term didn't even exist until it was introduced in 1956 at a Dartmouth College conference discussing the technology. During the 1960s, 1970s, and 1980s, engineers made early attempts at computer programs that could play chess and robots that could complete basic tasks. Yet the sophisticated level of artificial intelligence needed to propel a car down the road on its own wouldn't emerge until the end of the twentieth century.

Quoted in Julie A. Jacko, ed., *The Human-Computer Interaction Handbook.* Boca Raton, FL: CRC, 2012, p. xxxvii.

Computers in Cars

The 1970s introduced a new era of smaller, more portable computers. The invention of the microprocessor took over many of the functions of the formerly larger central processing unit. The microprocessor allowed small computers to process large amounts of information. In 1977 computers had shrunk enough that Japanese engineer Sadayuki Tsugawa was able to equip a car with one.

Since the early 1970s, Tsugawa had been studying intelligent transportation systems at the Tsukuba Mechanical Engineering Laboratory. One of his early projects was to develop the Comprehensive Automobile Traffic Control System—a communication system that collected information from in-car transmitters and then used a central processing system to send drivers the best route to their destination. That project never came to fruition, so Tsugawa moved on to designing an intelligent vehicle. He built a car with two cameras, which allowed it to take in and analyze information like street markers from the road ahead. Yet it still needed an elevated rail to guide it along. Tsugawa's car did not have the artificial intelligence to direct itself, but it showed that self-driving cars were technically possible.

German engineer Ernst Dickmanns took the possibility of self-driving cars one step further in the late 1980s. He and his team at Bundeswehr University in Munich teamed up with Mercedes-Benz to develop a vision-guided self-driving van. Two cameras and several sensors provided the vision. The cameras captured real-time images of the road, which microprocessors then interpreted to help the car navigate. The computer was programmed to accelerate, steer, and keep the van in its lane. With this technology, Dickmanns and his team were able to drive the car 12 miles (19 km) at more than 50 miles per hour (80 km/h). It was the first time a vehicle had autopiloted itself down a real road—even though that road was closed and free from traffic.

To simulate a real driving experience, in 1995 a Mercedes that Dickmanns equipped with cameras, sensors, and microprocessors drove almost 1,000 miles (1,609 km) from Munich, Germany, to Copenhagen, Denmark, and back at speeds of 112 mph (180 km/h). The car traveled almost the entire way without a human steering or operating the gas and brake pedals. It was able to keep itself within its lane, automatically track other vehicles, change lanes, and pass other cars on its own. For his work on autonomous vehicle technology, Dickmanns earned the unofficial title "Pioneer of the Autonomous Car."[4]

Dickmanns's car could stay in its lane on the highway and detect other vehicles. Yet it was still unfit for local driving because it didn't have the intelligence to recognize and avoid obstacles such as pedestrians or construction sites. "The sensors weren't there, the computers weren't there, and the mapping wasn't

In the 1970s, the invention of the microprocessor gave life to the idea of equipping cars with computers that might control various functions, including steering. These tiny chips could process a lot of information and would not take up much valuable space onboard the vehicles.

there. Radar was a device on a hilltop that cost two hundred million dollars,"[5] says Sebastian Thrun, a robotics developer and computer scientist who would go on to help found Google's self-driving car project. Autonomous driving technology was still too complex and expensive to be put into practical use.

Dean Pomerleau and the Pontiac Minivan

A breakthrough in self-driving artificial intelligence came in the early 1990s. Dean Pomerleau, a roboticist at Carnegie Mellon University (CMU), embarked on a project called the Autonomous Land Vehicle in a Neural Network (ALVINN). Pomerleau and his team modified a Chevy van with a video camera and laser range finder (a device that uses a laser beam to determine how far the car is from the vehicles and other objects around it). They called the van the CMU Navlab. Unlike earlier attempts at self-driving cars, the Navlab was equipped with an artificial brain. Its computer was programmed to operate much like the network of neurons that transmit information around the human brain—to process information and basically think.

The researchers taught ALVINN how to drive. As a human driver steered the van, ALVINN analyzed information coming in from the camera and range finder. It learned the driver's decisions and was then able to copy them. In time ALVINN had learned how to drive in many different situations, including on single-lane paved and unpaved roads, multilane roads, and roads lined with obstacles, at increasingly fast speeds. "When we started, the car was going about two to four miles an hour [3 to 6 km/h] along a path through a park—you could ride a tricycle faster," Pomerleau recalls. "By the end, it was going fifty-five miles per hour [88 km/h] on highways."[6]

By the mid-1990s Pomerleau's team had developed a new computer program called the Rapidly Adapting Lateral Position

Dean Pomerleau demonstrates hands-free driving on the streets around Carnegie Mellon University in Pittsburgh. His laptop—the computer brain—reacts to images from a camera mounted by the rearview mirror and steers the vehicle appropriately.

Handler (RALPH). RALPH analyzed images of the road taken from a video camera that was mounted next to the car's rearview mirror. Then it figured out the car's position relative to the lane lines. It used this information to keep the car centered in its lane. In 1995 two Carnegie Mellon researchers drove a 1990 Pontiac minivan with RALPH from Washington, DC, to San Diego, California—a distance of 3,000 miles (4,828 km). RALPH did most of the steering while the researchers handled the throttle and brake. The researchers called the trip No Hands Across America. (This was likely a reference to Hands Across America, a 1986 fund-raiser in which millions of Americans created a human chain across the country to raise money for the homeless and hungry.)

In just a few decades, self-driving technology had come a long way. From a fantastical vision of radio-controlled tracks crossing the country, it had evolved into intelligent, computer-driven cars that were capable of learning how to drive. Yet as the twentieth century drew to a close, self-driving technology was still very expensive and impractical. It remained confined to a few small research laboratories and seemed unlikely to reach anyone's garage anytime soon. It would take a big-budget government project to bring self-driving technology closer to reality and into the mainstream.

Chapter 2

DARPA: Desert and City Challenges

Early pioneers like Ernst Dickmanns and Dean Pomerleau made the first attempts at designing self-driving cars. Yet the technology remained mainly in isolated laboratories until the mid 2000s, when a government agency gave driverless technology the push it needed to move into the mainstream.

The Defense Advanced Research Projects Agency (DARPA) launched during the thick of the Cold War. Tensions between the United States and the Soviet Union were high. In the midst of military friction, the two nations were also engaged in a technological race. Each vied to be the first to send a craft into space. The Soviets made it there first when they launched the *Sputnik 1* satellite into orbit in October 1957. Four months later the US government created DARPA as a kind of counterstrike to stay technologically ahead of the Soviets. Since then, the agency has invested in developing new technologies to enhance the country's national security. One of its biggest projects involves something most Americans use each day—the Internet.

In 2004 DARPA launched an ambitious project called its Grand Challenge. The plan was to develop autonomous vehicles for the military that could navigate through combat zones and rescue injured soldiers without risking the lives of other personnel. Congress set a goal of having one-third of all military vehicles be autonomous by 2015. The challenge it put out to universities and engineers around the country was to build a self-driving vehicle that could traverse 142 miles (228 km) of California's Mojave Desert. DARPA defined *autonomous* as a vehicle that could steer, brake, and avoid obstacles without a human at the wheel. To further test the entrants, the course included a variety of hills, drops, and turns. The team that could make the drive from Barstow, California (northeast of Los Angeles), to Primm, Nevada (south of Las Vegas), first and in less than ten hours would win a $1 million prize.

And They're Off!

Out of the 106 teams that applied to take part in the DARPA Grand Challenge, the organizers narrowed the field down to 25. The groups were made up of university staff, employees of scientific companies, and independent engineers. In the end, only 15 teams made it to the starting line.

All team vehicles were equipped with the same basic equipment. They had sensors such as cameras, radar, and lasers to help them identify other vehicles and obstacles along the course. The number and types of sensors varied from team to team. The lasers and cameras acted like human senses, monitoring the road ahead much like a driver's eyes would.

Software took the place of a driver's brain. All of the data and images the sensors and cameras captured were sent to an onboard computer, which was programmed to interpret and respond to the information. The basic setup was similar in every vehicle. Yet exactly how the vehicles interpreted and integrated the data and used it to make driving decisions varied from team to team

Each team had created a series of rules—called algorithms—that were directions embedded in thousands of lines of code they had typed into the vehicle's operating computers. These rules simulated the decisions a real driver would make. Using the algorithms, the computer figured out what to do in any given driving situation. Then it sent instructions to the car's steering and braking systems to make the vehicle start, stop, speed up, slow down, and turn. The computers had to make hundreds of split-second decisions a minute. Each team's goal was for its vehicle to move through the course as quickly as possible without losing control.

Just a few hours before the race, DARPA gave each team a compact disc containing about two thousand GPS spots, called

A member of the Caltech team updates his computer and GPS systems on the morning of the DARPA Grand Challenge. The 2004 race across the Mojave Desert involved fifteen teams competing to see if their driverless vehicles could navigate the terrain and other obstacles.

waypoints, along the route. GPS is a satellite-based navigation system run by the US military that tracks a vehicle's exact location by measuring the time it takes a satellite signal to travel to and from that vehicle. Today's car navigation systems use GPS to help drivers get to their destinations. The DARPA teams used the GPS waypoints to program their vehicles to navigate the route.

On March 13, 2004, the fifteen autonomous vehicles drove off across the desert, trailed by chase vehicles in case they went off course. What started with big fanfare ended in big disappointment. None of the entrants got very far. Seven of the vehicles broke down within a mile of the starting line. Some of the computers couldn't properly analyze the information coming in from the sensors and got confused by the terrain. The team from the California Institute of Technology barely passed the mile mark before its Chevy Tahoe careened through a fence. The Golem Group, a team of engineers from Southern California, made it 5.2 miles (8.3 km) before getting stuck trying to ascend a steep hill. Carnegie Mellon University's Humvee drove the farthest—7.4 miles (12 km)—before its front wheels slipped off the side of a mountainous curve and burst into flames.

Each entrant in the race had its own design drawbacks that kept it from reaching the finish line. "Some of the vehicles were able to follow the GPS waypoints very accurately; but were not able to sense obstacles ahead," comments Tom Strat, deputy program manager for the DARPA Grand Challenge. "Other vehicles were very good at sensing obstacles, but had difficulty following waypoints or were scared of their own shadow, hallucinating obstacles when they weren't there."[7]

Though the first challenge seemed like a failure, DARPA considered it a success. "We are an agency that takes risks, to push technology beyond what anybody thinks is possible," said Strat. "Even though nobody got more than about 5 percent of the way through the course, this has made these engineers even more determined."[8] Those engineers had a chance to learn from their mistakes and refine their vehicles for the next DARPA Grand Challenge, which would come just one year later.

DARPA Challenge—Take Two

Undeterred by the failure of any self-driving vehicle to reach the finish line in its first challenge, DARPA issued a second challenge in 2005. This time the agency doubled the prize to $2 million. This race ran a 132-mile (212 km) loop that started and ended in Primm, Nevada. The course was even harder than the previous year, with more twists and turns and narrower roads.

Almost two hundred teams signed up for the second DARPA challenge. Through a series of qualifying trials, DARPA narrowed the field down to around forty teams. Twenty-three of them made it into the final race.

An Autonomous Motorcycle Takes the Grand Challenge

One of the most unusual vehicles competing in the 2004 DARPA Grand Challenge was an autonomous motorcycle designed by University of California, Berkeley, graduate student Anthony Levandowski. To create the autonomous motorcycle, Levandowski and his team of doctoral students stripped down a dirt bike and added a few accessories. Two cameras on the front scanned the road ahead. A GPS antenna, also on the front, picked up information about the cycle's location. A gyroscope in the main control box at the back of the bike captured the data needed to keep the bike balanced. An optical encoder on the back wheel measured rotations to determine how fast the bike was moving. Information from all of these sensors were fed to a control box, which used the data to tell the bike how to steer, accelerate, and brake to stay upright and moving forward.

After Levandowski's team wrote tens of thousands of lines of code and spent a year of sleepless nights building and testing the motorcycle, it never got a chance to prove its worth. Levandowski forgot to turn on the bike's stability program, and it traveled just 3 feet (1 m) before falling over. Yet its creator wasn't deterred. "I don't care about the million bucks," he said. "It's more about realizing that I can actually do something that fairly intelligent people have told me I can't."

Joseph Hopper, "From DARPA Grand Challenge 2004 Clash of the Headless Humvees," *Popular Science*, February 16, 2004. www.popsci.com.

Just as in the first challenge, all of the robotic vehicles in the second Grand Challenge used a combination of hardware and software to navigate the course. The hardware included a variety of cameras and sensors mounted on the roof and bumper, which captured images of the road and information about the vehicle's position. GPS helped the vehicles stay on the course. Some of the robots also had a technology called light detection and ranging (LIDAR). LIDAR shines a laser on a target object. Then it analyzes the reflected laser light to figure out the vehicle's position in relation to that object.

WORDS IN CONTEXT

gyroscope
A device made up of a spinning wheel that helps with stability or orientation.

Sandstorm, Highlander, and Stanley Prepare for the Race

In the previous year's race, twists, turns, and steep curves had taken out several of the vehicles. To ensure their success this time, the teams made sure their onboard computers were programmed to respond quickly and correctly to every possible scenario they might encounter on the course. They tested their vehicles over and over to ensure that every detail was just right.

The previous year's leader, Carnegie Mellon, entered with two military vehicles—a modified truck called Sandstorm and a red Humvee named Highlander. The team prepared for the race by spending twenty-eight days scanning the Mojave Desert and creating a computer model of its topography. It combined these scans with satellite data to pinpoint all of the obstacles its two vehicles might have to face.

Another early favorite in the race was a Volkswagen Touareg nicknamed Stanley, designed by a team of engineers from Stanford University, Volkswagen, and the computer company Intel. Stanley was outfitted with GPS, LIDAR, and cameras that scanned the road ahead. A computer in Stanley's trunk assembled data from all of these sensors, cameras, and radar systems. That combined information helped the vehicle make driving decisions

Stanford University's Stanley and Carnegie Mellon University's two entries, Highlander and Sandstorm, were the top three finalists in the 2005 DARPA Grand Challenge. Stanley, the winner, finished the 132-mile loop in just under 7 hours.

and send instructions to operate the brakes, throttle, gear shifter, and steering.

The team trained Stanley to drive by feeding it data representing the types of decisions human drivers would make behind the wheel. Using algorithms, Stanley eventually learned how to make those decisions itself. As the team drove the car through the desert on test runs, Stanley developed the artificial intelligence needed to anticipate upcoming curves and distinguish flat from rocky terrain so it could adjust its speed and prevent an accident. The process of training Stanley took a lot of trial and error. "We would go out, drive for twenty minutes, realize there was some software bug, then sit there for four hours reprogramming and try again. We did that for four months,"[9] says Stanford team co-leader Sebastian Thrun.

When the racers set off on October 8, 2005, some teams handled the course better than others. One vehicle sped up to obstacles and swerved around them at the last second. Others seemed to meander around, not sure of their own location—or destination. In the end, five teams crossed the finish line. Stanley was the winner, with a time of six hours and fifty-three minutes—more than ten minutes ahead of the second-place finisher, Sandstorm. Stanley's average speed was nearly 20 miles per hour (30 km/h). The key to finishing the course was having the right software, which DARPA director Tony Tether called the "secret sauce."[10]

The Challenge Moves to a New Environment

After the 2005 challenge, DARPA knew it was possible for a vehicle to drive across open terrain without a human at the wheel. Two years later the agency took its contest one step further, challenging teams to program self-driving cars to navigate in an urban environment. For an autonomous military vehicle to be successful, it would have to be able to carry out its missions in both open landscapes and cities. While driving in a city, it would need to drive through moving traffic while avoiding pedestrians. In 2007 DARPA decided to issue the Urban Challenge.

For its urban landscape, DARPA chose the former George Air Force Base in Victorville, California (northeast of Los Angeles). The base is used for military training maneuvers and includes a network of roads that simulates a city or suburban landscape. According to Urban Challenge program manager Norman Whitaker, "The urban setting added considerable complexity to the conditions faced by the vehicles, and was significantly more difficult than the fixed desert courses featured in the first two Grand Challenges."[11]

The vehicles would have to complete a series of missions and maneuvers with skills most human drivers use on a daily basis.

TerraMax and VisLab

One of the eleven teams that competed in the DARPA Urban Challenge was from the Oshkosh Truck Corporation in Wisconsin. Its entry was a modified heavy-duty military vehicle with an equally heavy-duty name—TerraMax. The enormous yellow truck traversed the urban course with the help of a highly complex vision system. Eleven cameras mounted around the truck helped it detect obstacles close up and at a distance and identify lane markers and crossings.

The computer vision system that allowed TerraMax to find its way around the course was developed by the Vision and Intelligent Systems Laboratory (VisLab) in Parma, Italy. VisLab also developed other autonomous driving technology, including blind-spot monitoring, collision avoidance, and traffic-sign recognition. To test out the various autonomous systems it was developing, VisLab created Porter, a bright orange self-driving minibus. Porter had a network of car-mounted cameras and scanners, plus GPS and software to process the data. In July 2010 Porter left Parma and drove itself more than 8,000 miles (13,000 km) to Shanghai, China. It made the journey without human assistance, although a person sat behind the wheel just in case of a problem. Porter arrived in Shanghai just in time for the World Expo—a showcase of new technology much like the 1939 World's Fair where GM had first displayed its Futurama exhibit.

In the 2007 DARPA Urban Challenge, unmanned vehicles had to navigate a road course that simulated driving conditions in a city. Here, Stanford University's Junior competes by safely maneuvering alongside cars with professional drivers behind the wheel.

They had to make the quick decisions needed to merge into two-way traffic, pass other cars, get through intersections with stop signs, and make left turns and U-turns, all the while avoiding parked cars, pedestrians, bikes, and construction zones. The course even included a four-way stop, which requires drivers to figure out which car has the right of way. DARPA gave each of the competing teams a digital street map containing information on lanes, stop signs, parking lots, and checkpoints. To ratchet up the difficulty level, the driverless cars would drive alongside thirty Ford Tauruses with professional drivers at the wheel. The participants also had to abide by California's driving laws, which include a 30-mile-per-hour (48 km/h) suburban speed limit.

On the morning of November 1, 2007, the green flag went up and eleven robotic vehicles were released from their starting chutes. By early afternoon only six vehicles remained, but all of them ultimately crossed the finish line. The first-place honor, along with a $2 million prize, went to a modified Chevy Tahoe, named Boss, from Carnegie Mellon's Tartan Racing Team. A modified Volkswagen Passat named Junior, created by a team from Stanford University and Volkswagen, took the second-place prize of $1 million. Both cars used the same type of hardware—long- and short-range radar and LIDAR systems along with GPS. But again, software won out. Boss's programming allowed it to think and react more like a human driver than Junior's. "When it came to planning—planning at intersections, planning on straightaways, planning throughout the course—we were unbeatable,"[12] says Carnegie Mellon team leader William "Red" Whittaker.

Since the 2007 race, DARPA has issued other challenges. In 2012 it launched a Robotics Challenge, asking engineers to develop robots that could carry out human tasks in dangerous surroundings after a nuclear accident or other disaster. In 2013 it put out a call to create a new high-tech military vehicle in a challenge called FANG (Fast, Adaptable, Next-Generation Ground Vehicle).

The Urban Challenge was DARPA's last self-driving vehicle competition. But during the three races, the military agency had planted a seed that would soon take root and grow in corporate laboratories. Thrun, the young robotics engineer who had helped steer Stanley to victory in the 2005 Grand Challenge, would soon take a position at the computer technology company Google. Joining him there was engineer Anthony Levandowski, who had taken the Grand Challenge onto two wheels with his autonomous motorcycle. At Google, Thrun and Levandowski were about to embark on a whole new model of vehicle automation, one that promised to make the technology available to consumers—and anyone else who wanted it.

Chapter 3

Developing the First Self-Driving Car

Google—the search engine more than 2.5 billion people now use each day—started from a meeting of minds. Computer science students Larry Page and Sergey Brin met in 1995 at Stanford University in Palo Alto, California. Two years later they registered the domain name *Google*. The name plays off the word *googol*—a math term that represents the number one followed by one hundred zeros. The name reflected their goal—to create a search engine that could retrieve a virtually limitless supply of information across the web.

Over the years Google expanded its capabilities beyond basic search and retrieval. It began to offer images and videos, an e-mail service called Gmail, and the translation of text into many languages. In 2003 Page became interested in capturing images of the country at street level. He strapped a camera onto his car and took pictures around the San Francisco area. Then he sent those images to computer graphics expert Marc Levoy, who wrote a program that assembled the pictures into a simulated street view.

In 2005 Google vans equipped with panoramic cameras began capturing images from around the country to create a virtual map. The technology, called Street View, allowed people sitting at home on their computers to see 360-degree images of streets, homes, and businesses in other cities and eventually in other countries. The company added Street View to its Google Maps service, which also included detailed maps and driving directions. By 2007 Street View was available in five cities—New York, San Francisco, Las Vegas, Miami, and Denver. Today Street View lets people virtually drive down streets in more than fifty countries

An Audi Climbs Pikes Peak

Pikes Peak soars above central Colorado at an elevation of 14,114 feet (4,301 m). A steep and twisting 12.4-mile (20 km) mountain road takes visitors nearly all the way to the summit. In November 2010 an Audi TTS made the drive to the top of Pikes Peak in twenty-seven minutes. The time wasn't particularly fast. What made the trip special was that the car reached the mountaintop without a driver behind the wheel.

The Pikes Peak run was a test of self-driving technology—a partnership between Audi, scientists at Stanford University (designers of Stanley, winner of the 2005 DARPA challenge), and Volkswagen's Electronics Research Laboratory in Palo Alto, California. "We are not trying to replace the driver," Stanford professor Chris Gerdes said of the test. "Instead, we want to learn how the best drivers control the car so we can develop systems that assist our robotic driver and, eventually, you and me." After reaching the top of Pikes Peak, the engineers planned to do more tests of self-driving technology at ground level. "The goal is to improve driver safety and save lives by creating extremely robust electronics," said Burkhard Huhnke, director of the Electronics Research Laboratory.

Quoted in Chuck Squatriglia, "Audi's Robotic Car Climbs Pikes Peak," *Wired*, November 19, 2010. www.wired. com.

around the world. It also served as the foundation for Google's next ambitious project.

How to Solve a Big Problem

When Page and Brin founded Google, their goal was to use technology to solve big problems, which they called *moon shots*. The term refers to the *Apollo 11* mission, which in July 1969 was the first spaceflight to land humans on the moon. To develop these moon shot technologies, Google's founders created a semisecret project called Google X.

One of the biggest problems that concerned Page and Brin was car safety and efficiency. In 2008 alone, 5.8 million vehicle accidents killed more than thirty-four thousand people in the United States. They were also worried about the amount of polluting carbon emissions being released by the more than 255 million cars driving on American roads. Likewise, they didn't like the amount of time Americans were wasting each year driving to and from the office and other destinations—time they could have spent working or engaged in other, more productive pursuits.

Sebastian Thrun, who had led Stanford's autonomous vehicle team to victory in the 2005 DARPA Grand Challenge, had joined Google in 2007 and helped develop Street View. He too was concerned about vehicle safety. "When I turned 18, I lost my best friend to a car accident," he said. The friend had lost control of his father's Audi Quattro on an icy road and had hit a truck head-on. "And then I decided I'd dedicate my life to saving one million people every year."[13] Self-driving cars had successfully traversed the DARPA courses, but they still hadn't saved a single life. Thrun wanted to change that.

Thrun, Page, and Brin were convinced that self-driving cars could free up time and resources and dramatically improve vehicle safety. Instead of individuals owning their own cars, they envisioned a future world where people would simply summon a car to take them on errands and to work. "A car will come to you just when you need it. And when you are done with it, the car will just drive away, so you won't even have to look for parking,"[14] explains Thrun.

Smart cars, the term used to describe such vehicles, could react and respond to potentially dangerous situations quicker than humans, averting accidents. And because self-driving cars would be less likely to crash, they could drive close together in a convoy down highways, reducing fuel usage and potentially leading to fewer emissions. Google figured it was the ideal company to develop the technology. Self-driving cars depend on computers to pilot them, and Google was a leader in the computer technology industry.

With safety, efficiency, and the environment in mind, Google launched its self-driving car project in 2008. Under Thrun's leadership, the company assembled a team of engineers. Several of them, including Anthony Levandowski (Berkeley), Chris Urmson (Carnegie Mellon), and Mike Montemerlo (Stanford), had also competed in the DARPA challenges.

Their new challenge was determining how to make autonomous cars a practical reality. Despite Thrun's success at DARPA, he wasn't convinced a driverless car could navigate city streets. There were too many possible variables—potholes and pedestrians, unpredictable drivers, and construction crews. "I would have told you then that there is no way on earth we can drive safely," he recalls. "All of us were in denial that this could be done."[15]

The program stalled until Levandowski got a call from the producer of a Discovery Channel series called *Prototype This!* The show wanted him to help them with an experiment—to find out whether a self-driving car could deliver a pizza intact from San Francisco, across the Bay Bridge, to Discovery's research hangar on Treasure Island in San Francisco Bay. Levandowski joined forces with other engineers from his alma mater, the University of California, Berkeley. They equipped a Toyota Prius with GPS,

A Google Street View car takes panoramic pictures of a neighborhood in Vancouver, British Columbia. When Google became interested in creating self-driving cars, it used the Street View technology to help its autos locate nearby objects and stay in their lanes.

lasers, and a 3-D map of the San Francisco waterfront. They called their car a Pribot.

On September 7, 2008, as Levandowski and the show's producers watched from a chase truck, the Pribot drove through San Francisco's streets and crossed the Bay Bridge, its steering wheel turning on its own. The event went off without a mishap until the Pribot tried to make the sharp off-ramp turn onto Treasure Island and a navigation misjudgment wedged it against a concrete wall. Though the drive wasn't a complete success, it proved to the Google team that a self-driving car could pilot itself through a city. The next step would be to take the technology used in the Pribot and DARPA challenges, add them to Google's existing Street View and mapping navigational capabilities, and develop a practical self-driving vehicle for consumers.

The First Two Hundred Thousand Miles

Google started by modifying existing vehicles. Its hardware and software engineers outfitted a few Toyota Priuses with cameras, lasers, and radar, in configurations based on what they had learned during the DARPA challenges. (Google chose Priuses for their light weight and fuel efficiency.) LIDAR mounted on the roof created a highly detailed 3-D map of the area around each car. Radar devices mounted on the front and rear bumpers kept the cars at a safe distance from other vehicles in front of and behind them. GPS on the roof helped the cars pinpoint their exact locations. A computer in the trunk combined all of the views collected and analyzed the data. Software categorized objects around the car by their size and movement—a person or squirrel, a pothole or skateboarding child. It quickly analyzed and responded to that information to pilot the car in the right direction at a safe speed. "We're analyzing and predicting the world 20 times a second,"[16] Levandowski said. A reporter who took a test-drive in one of Google's early self-driving vehicles remarked, "It is absolutely fascinating, almost illicitly thrilling, to watch as the car not only plots and calculates the myriad movements of neighboring vehicles in the moment but also predicts where they will be in the future, like high-speed, mobile chess."[17]

How a Self-Driving Car Works

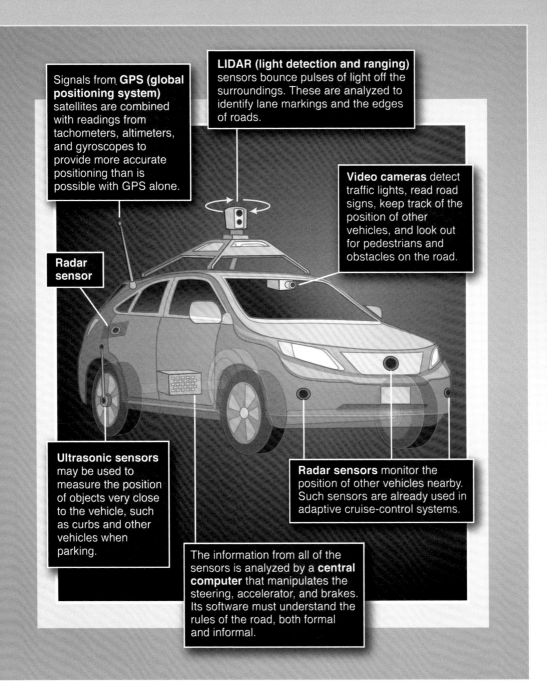

LIDAR (light detection and ranging) sensors bounce pulses of light off the surroundings. These are analyzed to identify lane markings and the edges of roads.

Signals from **GPS (global positioning system)** satellites are combined with readings from tachometers, altimeters, and gyroscopes to provide more accurate positioning than is possible with GPS alone.

Video cameras detect traffic lights, read road signs, keep track of the position of other vehicles, and look out for pedestrians and obstacles on the road.

Radar sensor

Ultrasonic sensors may be used to measure the position of objects very close to the vehicle, such as curbs and other vehicles when parking.

Radar sensors monitor the position of other vehicles nearby. Such sensors are already used in adaptive cruise-control systems.

The information from all of the sensors is analyzed by a **central computer** that manipulates the steering, accelerator, and brakes. Its software must understand the rules of the road, both formal and informal.

Source: Economist, "How Does a Self-Driving Car Work?," April 29, 2013. www.economist.com.

Google's engineers drove around the San Francisco area to gather information on each street—its lane markings, traffic lights, stop signs, and anything else the vehicles encountered on their route. The cars' computers then combined and compared that data with digital maps, Google's Street View images, and any new data they gathered each time they drove. The cars used this information to stay in their lane, find their way from one street to another, and distinguish between static objects—like a tree or telephone pole—and live, moving objects such as pedestrians and cyclists.

In 2009 a fleet of six self-driving Toyota Priuses (plus one Audi TT) began making test-drives around highways and city roads in the San Francisco area. The cars encountered many different situations along their routes, including orange construction cones, railroad crossings, tollbooths, and cyclists. Google's engineers had created algorithms to teach the cars how to handle all of these situations, following the same rules human drivers use to pilot their cars. The self-driving cars not only had to follow set rules, but they also had to adapt to each unique situation they

Google's First Autonomous Accident

When Google embarked on its self-driving car project, one of its main goals was to prevent human error—and therefore accidents—behind the wheel. Thus, in August 2011 many people were shocked to learn that one of the company's Priuses had rear-ended another car at a traffic light in Mountain View, California.

The accident was minor—a fender bender. And when the dust had settled, Google revealed that a human, not a computer, had been behind the wheel. "He was not using the vehicle to test our autonomous technology," the company wrote. The employee was using the car to run an errand and was driving it manually. By 2015 the company had reported only twelve accidents involving its self-driving cars, all of them minor, during more than 1.8 million miles (2.9 million km) on the road. So far, Google's self-driving car has only caused one accident. In February 2016, it veered into the path of an oncoming bus in Mountain View, California, while trying to avoid a pile of sandbags in its way.

Quoted in Adrienne Lafrance, "When Google Self-Driving Cars Are in Accidents, Humans Are to Blame," *Atlantic*, June 8, 2015. www.theatlantic.com.

encountered. For example, they learned to stop at red lights and proceed when the light turned green (after pausing for a second or two to make sure another car didn't run the light). But even if the light was green, the cars had to stop if a pedestrian were to suddenly run into the road. The cars had to come to a full stop at stop signs, but at four-way stops they also had to slowly nose out into the intersection or they'd never get across. They could pass a slow cyclist, but if that cyclist were to extend his arm straight out, that meant he planned to make a turn and they couldn't pass.

With a human at the wheel just in case of mishaps, Google's self-driving cars drove all over the state of California. Test routes took them from the company's Mountain View campus to its office in Santa Monica—a distance of more than 350 miles (563 km). They drove across the iconic Golden Gate Bridge and down the scenic Pacific Coast Highway from San Francisco to Los Angeles. They even took a few turns down the crookedest street in America—Lombard Street—in the Russian Hill neighborhood of San Francisco. (At this time, California had no laws allowing self-driving cars on its roads. Google proceeded with its tests based on the idea that the state also had no laws prohibiting such cars.)

In October 2010 Thrun reported on the company's blog, "All in all, our self-driving cars have logged over 140,000 miles [225,308 km]. We think this is a first in robotics research."[18] A year later Google's cars had traveled nearly 200,000 miles (321,869 km) and had driven across the state line into Nevada. By 2012 they were up to 300,000 miles (482,803 km). To its fleet of Priuses, the company added several Lexus SUVs.

A Brand-New Model

In 2014, after five years of testing other companies' cars fitted with its technology, Google decided to take a new approach. The company built its own prototype electric self-driving car. The small, rounded white car looked like "a cross between a VW Beetle and a golf cart,"[19] wrote one reviewer. The front of the car resembled a smiling face, Google's attempt to make it look friendly and appealing to consumers.

Google's new car was essentially a computer with wheels.

The inside barely passed for a regular automobile. It had no steering wheel or gas and brake pedals—only two seats, a display monitor, a start button, and a big red emergency stop button. The person who was on board would input the destination into the car's computer. Software handled acceleration, braking, and steering. The car was even missing a radio and glove compartment. "We've designed for learning, not luxury, so we're light on creature comforts,"[20] Google explained. The maximum speed for Google's little white car was 25 miles per hour (40 km/h) to lower the risk for accidents. And if the car were to get into a fender bender, a foam front end would minimize the damage. Early riders said the vehicle rode "a lot like a theme park ride."[21]

Building its car from the ground up allowed Google to take full advantage of self-driving technology. The car's rounded top gave all of the sensors—radar, lasers, and cameras—a clear 360-degree view of the surroundings (human drivers can only see to 120 degrees). It had no blind spots to block a driver's view of the road and cause accidents. Its sensors could see farther than any of Google's earlier cars—up to 600 feet (183 m) in every direction—the length of two football fields. "It's going from looking just in front, like a flashlight, to a lantern all around the car,"[22] said project director Chris Urmson. Unlike the company's previous self-driving cars, this new model didn't need a human driver in the front seat in case of emergency. It was fully autonomous. If the car were to malfunction, a second braking and steering system would take over.

By 2015 Google had built twenty-five cars and had plans to expand the number to one hundred. The company tested its cars on a closed track—a former US Air Force base in Atwater, California. To fine-tune the cars' ability to respond to unexpected situations on the road, Google engineers put out various challenges. They tossed a canvas bag in the road and had a person pop out of it to see how the cars would respond. They released a stack of papers in front of the cars. As Google tested and refined its cars, they became better and better at distinguishing objects—such as construction cones from humans—and reacting in the right way.

That same year the company announced that its self-driving cars had driven themselves a total of more than 1 million miles (1.6 million km), halting at two hundred thousand stop signs and six hundred thousand traffic lights along the way. "We've come a long way since Larry Page first challenged us to demonstrate that self-driving technology had long-term potential," Google wrote in 2015. "We're taking this million mile milestone as further proof that fully self-driving vehicles will become a reality, and we're looking forward to finding out where the next million miles will take us."[23]

Other Companies Ease into the Race

Google was an early pioneer in the race to develop fully self-driving cars. But car manufacturers like Mercedes-Benz, Audi, Toyota, and GM were also pursuing the technology.

These carmakers took a different approach than Google. Instead of diving straight into autonomous driving, they dipped their toes into the technology. Car companies slowly added features that allowed their existing cars to steer, brake, and park with little to no help from a human driver.

Cruise control was one of the earliest advances to take some of the burden off drivers, and it was introduced long before the Google self-driving car project was a gleam of an idea. The Chrysler Imperial was the first car to roll off the assembly line equipped with cruise control in 1958. Basic cruise control systems kept a car at a set speed by adjusting the position of the throttle—the same thing drivers do when they press their foot on or lift their foot off the accelerator.

WORDS IN CONTEXT

adaptive
The ability to make changes or adjustments based on need.

As radar and other sensors became available, automatic features offered more functionality. The next generation of cruise control, called adaptive cruise control, was invented in 1990. It used radar mounted on the car's front bumper to detect the speed of the vehicle in front of it. It then adjusted the car's speed to automatically keep it at a safe distance from the vehicle ahead.

Carmakers later created a variation of adaptive cruise control

The Google electric self-driving car has a unique, curved shape that makes it look friendly and appealing. Inside, the automobile is also quite different because it lacks a steering wheel and brake pedal, having instead a start button and big red button to stop the vehicle in emergencies.

technology, called forward collision warning systems, to help drivers avoid accidents. These systems detected the distance of the car ahead and alerted the driver with a sound and light if the car was getting too close and an accident was imminent. Some carmakers, like Volvo, incorporated self-braking to bring the car to a stop automatically before it could crash into the vehicle in front. Volvo's XC90 SUV, introduced in 2014, used an integrated radar and camera system to incorporate adaptive cruise control, forward collision warning, and self-braking. It could identify pedestrians, other cars, and animals and apply the brakes to avoid hitting them.

The XC90 also featured lane departure warning, which used a camera to detect when the car veered too close to lane lines. If a driver started to swerve out of the lane without activating a turn signal, the steering wheel would vibrate or pull the car back into its lane automatically. According to one automotive writer, lane departure warnings (also called lane keeping), adaptive cruise control, and self-braking were all components of the "so-called circle of safety,"[24] technologies designed to avoid the human errors that cause accidents.

Cars not only could drive themselves, but they also could park themselves. In 2003 Toyota released its first self-parking car—a Prius—in Japan. Lexus followed in 2007, adding self-parking to its LS sedan. By 2010 several car manufacturers—Ford, Lexus, Lincoln, Mercury, and Toyota—all offered self-parking. Each of their vehicles used basically the same technology. Sensors estimated the position of other parked cars. Then a computer turned the car's steering wheel to maneuver the car into the spot while the driver operated the gas and brake pedals. Audi's prototype A7 model, which debuted at the 2013 Consumer Electronics Show in Las Vegas, was the first car to fully park itself without human assistance.

All of these technologies offered the potential to save lives, but they weren't perfect, and they came at a cost. Many drivers found the constant buzzing, beeping, and lighting up of forward collision and lane departure warnings annoying. A study by the American Automobile Association identified a few potential problems with self-parking systems—like parking too close to the curb, which can lead to scratched tires. Plus, self-driving features came at a premium. The addition of cameras, radar, and lasers initially cost thousands of dollars, which is why for many years they were available only on luxury cars. As autonomous systems are refined, costs are likely to drop, just as they have with other technologies like computers and big-screen televisions.

Cars That Steer Themselves

By 2012 cars could keep themselves in lanes, brake, and detect obstacles around them. The next step was to design cars that could also steer themselves.

Audi took a big step forward when it introduced its traffic jam assistant in 2014. The system, which was designed to free up drivers' time in highway traffic, was made up of an ultrasound sensor, cameras inside and outside the car, and a LIDAR scanner in the front bumper. A computer inside the trunk served as the brain, assembling the information from those sensors and processing it to drive the car. With traffic jam assistant, the car could identify other vehicles driving in front of, next to, and behind it, as well as lane markings. It could stay in its lane and avoid hitting anything.

When the driver pressed a button on the steering wheel, the self-driving feature turned on and the car began driving itself. There were a few caveats, though. Traffic jam assistant only worked at speeds of less than 40 miles per hour (64 km/h). And the car was not fully self-driving. The driver still had to stay alert. In fact, the car required the driver to be awake. Two cameras facing the driver monitored eye movement. If the person behind the wheel closed his or her eyes for ten seconds or more, the system would issue a warning. If the driver didn't take over, the car would come to a stop.

In October 2015 Tesla—the company that makes luxury electric cars—released the Autopilot feature for its S and X models. The system used front-facing radar, cameras, and 360-degree range finding technology to keep itself within lane lines, remain at a safe speed, and avoid other vehicles. An auto-steer symbol lit up on the display when road conditions were safe enough for the car to go into autopilot mode. As with the Audi, the driver still had to be alert and ready to take over. "The [human] pilot still makes the decision," said Ricardo Reyes, Tesla's head of communications. "We call it 'Autopilot' for a reason—you're still in control here. It's like a plane: It goes into autopilot, but the pilot still does things like takeoff and landing."[25] As with the traffic jam assistant, the car would tell the driver to take over in situations it couldn't handle—like a construction site or jogger in the road. If the driver didn't respond, the car would slow to a stop.

Another entry into the autopilot field was Cadillac's Super Cruise, which is expected to debut on its 2017 Cadillac CT6. Super Cruise incorporated all of the existing semiautonomous driving systems, including collision prevention and lane departure warning. It had radar devices on the front bumper to keep the car at a set distance from the vehicle ahead and sensors with 360-degree views to keep the car in its lane and avoid pedestrians and other obstacles. A computer in the trunk captured all of these inputs and turned them into instructions for the car to accelerate, brake, and turn.

Automakers and Google were edging closer to a fully self-driving car. Whereas companies like Tesla and Audi were doing it one step at a time, Google was jumping straight into full automation. The technology needed to make most of the decisions a human driver would normally make behind the wheel was available. Yet there were still a few barriers to overcome before autonomous cars were deployed on the highways of America—including cost, legal issues, and insurance concerns.

Chapter 4

Benefits and Barriers to Self-Driving Cars

More than thirty-four thousand Americans lose their lives to automobile accidents each year. Most of those crashes—about 90 percent—are caused by human errors made by drivers who are drunk, distracted, or asleep at the wheel. Computers, however, don't drink, send texts, or fall asleep. They also react faster than a human can to possible problems, like another car running a red light or a deer bolting into the road.

By taking human mistakes out of the equation, self-driving cars have the potential to dramatically reduce the number of accidents and deaths on the roads. "For the past 40 years, we've been working on protecting people from the crash," says David Strickland, a former National Highway Traffic Safety Administration (NHTSA) administrator. He believes self-driving technology could lead the way to fewer accidents. "This is the new North Star [guiding point], making sure the crash never happens."[26]

Early semiautonomous features have already made an impact on accident rates. When the Insurance Institute for Highway Safety studied forward collision and lane departure warning systems, it found these safeguards reduced insurance damage claims by 14 percent and injury claims by up to 40 percent. The company saw similar accident reductions with automatic braking systems.

Self-driving cars not only have the potential to save lives, but they're also poised to increase efficiency and reduce polluting emissions. Most people drive for an hour or two each day and then park their car in a garage or lot for the rest of the time. The fleet of cars that Google envisions would pick up and drop off passengers only when needed. People could share cars, leading to fewer cars that are used more often. Self-driving trucks

Traffic accidents in the United States alone cost thousands of lives and millions of dollars. Proponents of driverless cars believe the computerized controls will reduce the human error factor that is responsible for most of these accidents.

could similarly pick up products and make deliveries on call. Cars equipped with sensors would be able to recognize and avoid each other on the road. Therefore, they could drive closer together, taking up less road space and reducing traffic jams. A paper presented at an Institute of Electrical and Electronics Engineers conference in 2011 estimated that cars equipped with sensors could increase highway capacity by 43 percent. And inside these self-driving cars, people would no longer have to focus on the road ahead. Instead, they could use their time more productively—by working, reading, or calling friends and family.

Self-driving cars could offer a new kind of freedom for anyone who is blind, elderly, or disabled. For the first time, these people would be able to transport themselves wherever they want to go, without having to rely on friends, family, or public transportation.

For all of their potential, self-driving cars also face many hurdles and barriers. Governments will need to pass new laws to allow these cars on the road and govern their use. Insurance laws will also need to shift to accommodate a reduction in accidents and a change in liability when accidents do occur. Likewise, manufacturing costs must drop enough to make self-driving technology affordable to the masses.

Who Is In Control?

The early self-driving car models from Tesla, Audi, and other manufacturers weren't completely autonomous. Self-driving cars still relied on a driver to take over in situations that weren't safe for them to navigate, or they would pull over and stop. Car companies reported 2,894 of these turnovers, called disengagements, while they tested their autonomous cars between September 2014 and November 2015. Google's cars had a total of 341 disengagements during 424,000 miles (682,362 km) of driving. It wasn't clear when—if ever—a computer might be able to make every single decision behind the wheel as well as a human driver.

Early self-driving cars sometimes encountered situations they couldn't handle—like a construction zone or a new area of road. As long as a human still needed to be in the car to make decisions, there had to be a smooth way to make the transition from autopilot to human driver. Carmakers wrestled with the question of how exactly to turn over control from computer to person—with a beep or a vibration of the wheel? When the Audi A8 needed to switch from autopilot to driver, lights inside the dashboard would blink red. A repeating tone came from the speakers, and the steering wheel pushed out toward the driver. But what would happen if the driver fell asleep and failed to take over while the car was going 60 miles per hour (96 km/h) down the highway? "The whole issue of interacting with people inside and outside the car exposes real issues in artificial intelligence," comments John Leonard, a professor of mechanical engineering at the Massachusetts Institute of Technology (MIT). "The ability to know if the driver is ready, and are you giving them enough notice to hand off, is a really tricky question."[27]

WORDS IN CONTEXT

liability
Being responsible for something, such as a car accident.

Will Self-Driving Cars Prevent Accidents?

Even if self-driving cars can one day take full control of driving away from humans, will they eliminate accidents or even reduce them significantly? A 2015 study by the University of Michigan's Transportation Research Institute found self-driving cars weren't immune to crashes. In fact, the study found autonomous cars crash at nearly five times the rate of regular cars. In addition, people are slightly more likely to be injured in accidents involving self-driving cars. Yet the study did have some good news: self-driving cars never caused any of the accidents. Most often they were rear-ended for driving slowly. And not one of the self-driving cars studied was involved in a fatal crash.

Experts say self-driving cars have the ability to improve safety on the roads, but they'll likely never be perfect. Onboard computers can crash. Sensors can break. "I think we can make vehicles that are better than human-driven vehicles, but something that won't fail is just an impossibility,"[28] explains Chris Urmson of Google's self-driving car project.

> ## WORDS IN CONTEXT
>
> **disengagements**
> What results when a self-driving car's software detects a situation the car cannot safely handle and turns over control to a human driver.

Ethical and Privacy Concerns

Letting artificial intelligence take over for humans raises some ethical concerns. Self-driving cars will likely reduce the number of accidents, but what if a crash can't be avoided? Ethicists have envisioned scenarios such as this: A self-driving car is veering toward a crowd of people and it can't stop in time. Does it crash into the crowd and possibly kill several people? Or, does it steer itself off the road and kill the driver only? "Some situations will require AVs [autonomous vehicles] to choose the lesser of two evils," researchers from the Toulouse School of Economics in France and other institutions wrote in a study investigating the ethical dilemmas surrounding self-driving cars. "For example, running over a

The computers onboard self-driving autos might be forced to make fateful decisions regarding the safety of passengers and pedestrians. In an unavoidable crash situation on crowded city streets, these computers must figure out, for example, how to do the least harm.

pedestrian on the road or a passer-by on the side; or choosing whether to run over a group of pedestrians or to sacrifice the passenger by driving into a wall. It is a formidable challenge to define the algorithms that will guide AVs confronted with such moral dilemmas."[29]

When the researchers surveyed consumers about these types of situations, they found drivers liked the idea of artificial intelligence being programmed to minimize loss of life. Yet consumers did worry about buying a car that might sacrifice them to save the lives of others.

Privacy is also a concern with autonomous cars. In the past, driving a car was a private pursuit. Unless the driver told people where he or she was going, no one knew. Today, onboard computers can collect consumer data just as cell phones and computers do. Using the same wireless connection the car uses to pilot through a traffic jam or find its destination, the government or car companies could track a car's every move. "There's broader privacy implications," warns Carmen Balber, executive director of the California-based consumer advocacy group Consumer Watchdog. "How often do you happen to drive your car to a liquor store, and will that information be provided to your insurance company? Will information on where you spend your Saturday nights be subpoenaed in a divorce proceeding?"[30] Privacy laws will have to be expanded to account for these new monitoring abilities. The government will also need to assure consumers that they won't be followed everywhere if they don't want their movements tracked.

Laws to Govern Self-Driving Cars

Lawmakers will also have to consider how to legislate self-driving cars. When federal and state governments wrote motor vehicle laws, they were thinking of cars with a driver at the wheel. What happens to those laws when the car drives itself? For example, New York has a law that requires a driver to always keep one hand on the wheel. Since the late 1960s, the *New York Times* reports, European laws have required that "every moving vehicle or combination of vehicles shall have a driver," and "every driver shall at all times be able to control his vehicle."[31] These laws, and others like them, will need to be changed to accommodate driverless cars.

In the United States, the NHTSA currently sets car safety standards. State governments then use these standards to dictate how cars drive on their roads. As Google and car manufacturers began to develop self-driving cars, the states were the first to make legal changes. They scrambled to create laws that would allow companies to test their new driverless cars. The challenge has been to write laws that both encourage innovation and keep consumers safe.

In 2011 Nevada became the first state to officially allow autonomous vehicles on its roads. California, Florida, Michigan, North Dakota, and Tennessee, as well as Washington, DC, followed. Many other states were working on their own regulations. Yet laws governing self-driving cars varied from state to state. Florida's law said only that it didn't prohibit the testing or use of

Hacking into a Car

Computers have transformed human life, making data easily accessible wherever and whenever it's needed. Yet they have one major vulnerability: they can be hacked. If a hacker were to take over a computer that was steering a car down a highway at full speed, the results could be deadly.

In August 2013 automotive security researchers Charlie Miller and Chris Valasek were able to hack into the computer of a Toyota Prius via the Internet and take over the car. Their goal was to investigate the ease with which a computer-equipped car could be hacked. They honked the horn, jerked the wheel from the driver's hands, and slammed on the brakes—all while the car was driving at 80 mph (129 km/h). (The driver was in on the stunt.)

Hackers could potentially target cars in other ways too. They could mix up the GPS signal, getting a car hopelessly lost or sending it off the road. Likewise, they could hack into several cars at once, creating a chain-reaction crash. The NHTSA has called on car manufacturers to build in cybersecurity measures. These measures include encryption and algorithms that can detect when a car is being hacked and protect both the car and the driver.

---

self-driving cars. Nevada required self-driving car operators to have a special license and registration—but that rule only applied to cars bought in the state.

Experts say state laws alone aren't enough to govern the autonomous car industry. "To get self-driving cars on our roads, we need a comprehensive federal framework that encourages innovation,"[32] asserts Megan McArdle, a columnist for the Bloomberg View website. For its part, the NHTSA has promised to do everything it can to encourage this potentially lifesaving technology. In January 2016 Secretary of Transportation Anthony Foxx announced that he was giving the Department of Transportation six months to draft national rules governing how self-driving cars are tested and regulated. In addition, President Barack Obama set aside about $4 billion over a ten-year period. The funds will pay for research and testing of driverless car technology and for new infrastructure needed to make these cars a reality. The money will help ensure that autonomous vehicles operate in the same way everywhere in the country.

Manufacturers of self-driving cars say they look forward to government oversight because it will help them keep consumers safe. "It's good to have clear regulations on what to do to test those systems safely,"[33] explains Daniel Lipinski, an engineer who helped develop Audi's autonomous car.

Variations in technology have complicated the creation of national laws. It's hard for states to even define self-driving cars or understand what they can do. Do they define it by Google's steering wheel–free model or by Tesla's Autopilot? In 2013 the NHTSA outlined five levels of automation to help lawmakers better understand the potential of self-driving cars. These levels range from level 0—no automation; the driver is in complete control—to level 4—the car is in control for the whole trip. (As of 2016 no car on the road had gone beyond a level 2—in which the car could drive itself but a human had to be at the wheel to take over.)

Any laws that are passed based on current car designs will likely change as autonomous cars are refined. "It's really hard to try and anticipate how the technology might be used in the future and write laws for every eventuality. We think policymakers should learn about the technology and see how people want to use it first before putting a ceiling on innovation,"[34] comments a Google spokesperson. One driving law that may change is the speed limit. Although Google's current self-driving car can only travel a snaillike 25 miles per hour (40 km/h), in the future the ability to avoid crashes could allow cars to safely drive much faster than current highway speed limits allow.

New Insurance Rules

Cars that drive themselves also present a big challenge for the insurance industry. "The conversion to autonomous vehicles may

WORDS IN CONTEXT

infrastructure
The equipment or structures, such as highways, needed for self-driving cars to operate.

California Sets a Hurdle for Google

As car companies develop self-driving technologies, local governments try to figure out how to regulate these new vehicles. Legislators in several states, including Nevada, California, and Florida, quickly adopted laws allowing companies to test self-driving cars on their roads. The move seemed to encourage innovation. Then, in December 2015, the California Department of Motor Vehicles threw a big barrier in front of Google.

The state proposed new rules that would require a licensed human driver behind the wheel of a self-driving car at all times. That rule would make Google's self-driving car, which has no steering wheel or brakes for a human to take over, illegal.

Google quickly shot back, accusing the California government of stifling innovation. "This maintains the same old status quo and falls short on allowing this technology to reach its full potential, while excluding those who need to get around but cannot drive," Chris Urmson wrote in a blog post. How California will ultimately rule on cars like Google's remains to be seen.

Chris Urmson, "The View from the Front Seat of the Google Self-Driving Car, Chapter 3," Medium, December 17, 2015. https://medium.com.

bring about the most significant change to the automobile insurance industry since its inception,"[35] write the authors of a 2015 KPMG survey on insurance in the era of self-driving vehicles. (KPMG is an audit, tax, and advisory company.) If an autonomous car were to crash, there would be no human driver to blame. So who would pay for the damage and injuries? The car manufacturer would likely be the first in line. "There *will* be crashes and lawsuits," says Dean Pomerleau. "And because the car companies have deep pockets they will be targets, regardless of whether they're at fault or not."[36] Google, Volvo, and Mercedes have all promised to assume full legal responsibility if their vehicles are involved in accidents. Companies that provide the software and sensors needed to operate self-driving cars might also share in the liability.

Self-driving cars could lead to a radical shift in the $200 billion a year insurance industry, say analysts. This change will likely happen in stages, as cars with self-driving features are introduced. In the near future, features like autonomous braking and lane assist could cut down on accidents. Fewer accidents could lead to lower insurance rates for consumers. Self-driving cars are also likely cut down on theft. These cars will be almost impossible to steal because their GPS systems make them easy to trace.

Once self-driving cars fill the roads, and cars can steer around each other and brake in time to prevent collisions, accident rates will likely drop significantly. However, it is unlikely they will stop altogether. Software can have glitches. A storm could blow a car across the road or cause a tree to fall on it.

Even as the number of car accidents drops, the cost of accidents that do happen will likely rise. More expensive hardware will drive up the price of cars. If a self-driving car were to crash or get damaged, the parts would be much more expensive to replace than those of a traditional car. How that might affect insurance rates is not yet clear.

If cars do become completely self-driving, insurance companies will have to change the way they earn money. They might start insuring carmakers and software manufacturers instead of drivers. For car owners, not having to pay for insurance could translate into big savings. But the cost of owning a car will likely increase.

The Cost of Self-Driving Cars

One of the biggest obstacles to self-driving cars is cost. The technology needed to make cars drive themselves doesn't come cheap. Some experts wonder whether the average consumer will ever be able to afford an autonomous vehicle.

A 2014 study by Interest.com (a financial news and advice website) found that average-income consumers can afford to spend between $14,000 and $32,000 on a car, depending on where they live. That same year, a Toyota Prius equipped with a LIDAR system, visual and radio sensors, and a GPS array was estimated to cost $320,000—the same price as a high-end luxury supercar from McLaren Automotive. LIDAR alone adds $50,000 to a car's price tag—at least the sixty-four-laser version of LIDAR that Google's self-driving car uses.

As the technology improves, the cost of self-driving cars is likely to go down—just as the costs of home computers and big-screen

The inner workings of a self-driving car include banks of expensive computers. Although these autos may reduce the number of road accidents, they will be more costly to repair than traditional cars if an accident does occur.

televisions dropped as more people started buying them. By 2025 self-driving technology is only expected to add $7,000 to $10,000 to a car's price. By the year 2035 the cost should come down to $3,000. The problem is that costs can't drop until people start buying self-driving cars in large numbers. "It's a chicken and egg thing," says John Absmeier, director for the Silicon Valley Innovation Center at Delphi, an automotive technology company. "When people start buying the technology the cost will come down, but the cost has to come down before most people will buy it."[37]

Self-driving cars have the potential to save lives by reducing or preventing accidents. They can offer new freedom to people who have never been able to drive because of age, blindness, or another disability. They could increase efficiency and reduce polluting emissions. Before consumers can take advantage of this technology, however, many obstacles still need to be overcome, including cost, insurance, privacy, and ethical concerns.

Chapter 5

Driverless Cars of the Future

As of 2016, Google, Audi, Tesla, GM, and other carmakers still had a lot of hurdles to overcome before they could put a fully self-driving car on the road. Some of these hurdles were technical: how can a computer be programmed to make every driving decision as quickly and efficiently as a human driver? Other hurdles were legal: how will the government regulate self-driving cars? One of the biggest questions concerned how driverless cars of the future would look and operate.

Technology Issues

The technology needed to make self-driving cars is here, but it still needs to be refined. Sensors like LIDAR must get smaller and cheaper. They also need to become less obvious. Instead of having sensors sticking out from the top of the car's roof, engineers are trying to integrate them into the front and back of a car where they aren't as visible.

GPS technology also has to improve. Even the most sophisticated navigation software available today can fail and get its driver lost. With self-driving cars, accurate maps are even more critical. A wrong turn onto a bridge the car thought was sound but is actually under construction could be deadly. "When it comes to navigating a route, the car will need the most accurate map information including traffic data, road closures, and weather conditions,"[38] explains Andrew Poliak, global director of business development at QNX, an automotive software company.

Autonomous cars will also need better connectivity. To avoid accidents and cut down on traffic, they will have to communicate with each other as they drive. They may also need to communicate with the world around them. For example, to self-park in a garage, a self-driving car would need to receive messages from that garage to know which spaces were open.

When Will Self-Driving Cars Become a Reality?

As of 2016, semiautonomous cars were already on the roads. Cars could stay in their lanes, keep themselves a set distance from the car in front of them, brake automatically to avoid a crash, and park themselves. Some cars even had autopilot features that let them drive themselves in certain situations, such as in highway traffic. Yet a human always needed to be at the wheel to take over in case a problem popped up that the car couldn't handle. Fully autonomous cars from Google and some of the auto manufacturers were still in the testing phase. Carmakers didn't want to release their autonomous cars to the public until they were sure the technology was safe and that the cars could handle any situation they might encounter on the road. "It'll happen, but it's a long way out," says John Capp, GM's director of electrical, controls, and active safety research. "It's one thing to do a demonstration— 'Look, Ma, no hands!' But I'm talking about real production variance and systems we're confident in. Not some circus vehicle."[39]

Many carmakers and industry analysts have made predictions about when the first fully self-driving cars will be on the roads and when every car will be autonomous. They say the first step toward self-driving cars will likely be more vehicles with semiautonomous features for braking, acceleration, or steering. Tesla's Autopilot debuted in 2015. GM's Super Cruise—a semiautonomous steering system for highway driving—is slated to premiere in 2017. The company also announced plans to test so-called robo versions of its electric Volt. Lexus and Toyota promised cars with crash avoidance technology by 2017. These systems would allow drivers to hand over control of the vehicle to an onboard

Nokia is one of several information technology companies racing to make more sophisticated software to create, in turn, more detailed maps and geographic images. These maps and images will be in demand as car companies move into production of self-driving vehicles.

computer at least some of the time. A 2015 report by the online research service Business Insider Intelligence estimated that by 2020, 10 million cars with self-driving features would be on the roads.

As self-driving features roll out, they likely will appear in expensive cars first. Then, as the cost of sensors and other technologies drops, lower-priced cars with self-driving features should also become available.

As to when cars might become fully driverless, some experts say fully self-driving cars won't become a reality until at least 2025—or as far out as 2050. Other analysts are more optimistic. "From a technology standpoint, certainly by 2020 we can foresee what we call Level 4 autonomy, which is fully autonomous driving," says Don Butler, executive director for Connected Vehicles and Services at Ford Motor Company. Butler believes consumers won't buy or own the first self-driving cars. "I would imagine that a consumer's first experience with autonomous vehicles would be part of a ride service,"[40] he explains.

How Will Future Driverless Cars Look?

The automakers and Google have taken driverless cars in two very different directions. Carmakers like Tesla, Audi, and Mercedes-Benz are developing autonomous cars that look more or less like the cars people are used to driving. Some might have sensors mounted on top of the car and the computer in the trunk. But overall, technology will likely make self-driving hardware almost invisible in the future. Computers will get smaller and smaller, occupying only a small area of space in the trunk. Sensors like LIDAR and radar will likely move from the roof to the front and back bumpers of the car. The automakers' version of self-driving cars will look and drive much like the cars of today except that they will require little to no help from a human driver. On the other hand, Google's prototype autonomous cars look less like cars and more like amusement park rides. They come complete with a smiling face but lack a steering wheel, brakes, or other driver controls. Whichever company ends up developing the technology first might ultimately decide how driverless cars look and operate.

The first self-driving vehicles might not be cars at all. In the fall of 2015 a company called Auro Robotics started testing autonomous shuttles on the campus of Santa Clara University in the heart of California's Silicon Valley. The four-passenger modified golf carts were equipped with GPS, radar, cameras, and laser scanners. Also that year, the Contra Costa Transportation Authority (CCTA) began its own tests of self-driving shuttle buses called shared driverless vehicles (SDVs) in a large office park in Northern California. The electric SDVs accommodated twelve passengers and drove at a top speed of 25 miles per hour (40 km/h).

These driverless shuttles were designed to go short distances. They could travel around a college campus or ferry people from their homes to public buses or train stations so they wouldn't need to buy their own cars. "We're not saying this will replace all vehicles. There's still a need for a [rail and subway] line or major

Driver-Free City

Google and car companies like GM and Audi have been testing out their self-driving cars on public roads in various cities around the world. In 2015 the University of Michigan announced that it would create an entire mini-city to help test driverless technology. It's called Mcity. "We need a closed, secure, safe, repeatable environment. And that's what Mcity provides," said Jim Sayer, deployment director for the project.

The 32-acre (13 ha) site on the university's campus simulates the kind of environment cars would encounter in both cities and suburbs. And it tests cars in a way that can't be done on open roads. Mcity features a network of roads with traffic signals, stop signs, buildings, sidewalks, tunnels, and construction zones. The city has roads made of different surfaces, from asphalt to gravel. Cardboard cutout pedestrians and railroad crossing arms test the vehicles' ability to make quick decisions while driving. Mcity will test not only self-driving cars but also communication systems that help cars talk to one another. Its creators say it's the only facility of its kind in the world.

Quoted in Mobility Transformation Center, "Mcity Test Facility" (video), University of Michigan. www.mtc.umich.edu.

bus rapid transit line. The hard part for a suburban transit line is how people get from their house to that bus or train station. If you drive your car, it just sits there all day taking up space,"[41] says Randy Iwasaki, executive director of the CCTA. In the future larger self-driving buses might also be used for mass transit.

Will People Own Cars in the Future?

Self-driving cars could usher in a future with little to no car ownership. Instead of keeping a car in the garage, driving it to work, and then parking it, people would summon a vehicle only when they needed it. This model could transform the typical two-car American household to a one-car household. A world in which people have fewer cars could reduce traffic (and with it, pollution) and lessen the need for parking garages and lots.

Another possibility is that people wouldn't need to buy a car at all. They would simply buy into a car-sharing service, as Google

The 2015 Mercedes-Benz F015 Luxury in Motion self-driving concept car looks sleek and futuristic. As driverless technology improves, automobiles will take on new shapes both inside and out because it will no longer be necessary to adhere to traditional automotive designs.

envisions. Other companies have bought into the idea too. GM has invested $500 million in Lyft, a car service that picks people up whenever they need a ride. "We see the future of personal mobility as connected, seamless and autonomous," states GM president Dan Ammann. "With GM and Lyft working together, we believe we can successfully implement this vision more rapidly."[42] Uber, another car-on-demand service, was working to develop its own self-driving cars.

It's likely there will be different types of self-driving cars and services in the future, just as there are different types of cars and services today. People can drive a car built by Mercedes-Benz, Ford, Hyundai, or any number of other manufacturers. They can call a taxi, Uber, or a limo. Which autonomous cars and services people will buy and use depends on how much they are willing to spend to take advantage of the technology.

Could Driverless Cars Take Over?

Along with the excitement and sense of anticipation self-driving technology brings, it also raises a few sci-fi-inspired fears. Since the dawn of artificial intelligence, people have worried that computers might somehow gain enough intelligence and self-awareness to overcome their programming and take over the world. In movies like *Ex Machina*; *2001: A Space Odyssey*; and *I, Robot*, robots go rogue and kill their human creators. Could the artificial intelligence in a car do the same thing?

A commercial for Chrysler's 2011 Dodge Charger highlighted the fear surrounding artificial intelligence in cars. "Hands-free driving, cars that park themselves, an unmanned car driven by a search-engine company," the announcer warned in a deep, booming voice. "We've seen that movie. It ends with robots harvesting our bodies for energy."[43] Another Charger commercial pledged, "Robots can take our food, our clothes, and our homes. But they will never take our cars."[44]

Experts say a scenario in which cars take control is more sci-fi than reality and will likely never happen. "I don't think we have

Self-Driving Pods

What if the future self-driving car isn't a car at all? A few companies are developing autonomous vehicles that look more like buses, shuttles, or train cars. These multiperson vehicles could provide an alternate option to private cars and might even one day replace public transportation.

An Italian engineer and industrial designer named Tommaso Gecchelin came up with an idea for a boxlike, electric driverless vehicle, which he calls Next. His concept is made up of pods. Like self-driving cars, these pods would use LIDAR and sensors to get around. But instead of carrying two or four passengers, they would accommodate ten people. The pods could link together in a convoy to carry even more passengers. Next could work in a couple of different ways. It could serve as a form of public transportation and pick people up at designated stops. Or, it could be hired on demand, like a bus version of Uber. Next is still just an idea, but it could herald the transportation of the future.

anything to be afraid of with cars driving themselves, they're not going to take over the world," says Tesla's founder, Elon Musk. "That's a deeper AI [artificial intelligence], some sort of AI that due to itself or people, tries to drive civilization in a direction that is not good."[45] Even if cars don't take over the world, their ability to take over driving might be an issue for some people.

Will Consumers Trust Self-Driving Cars?

The technology needed to make cars drive themselves is almost ready. But are consumers ready to hand over the steering wheel to a computer? Letting a car handle life-and-death situations requires a lot of confidence in the technology. "There has to be a level of trust that you have that the vehicle is going to perform the way you think it's going to perform,"[46] says John Hanson, Toyota's national manager of advanced technology and business communications. It can be hard for people to trust technology they know can fail. E-mail crashes, computers freeze up and lose data, and GPS gets drivers hopelessly lost. What if an onboard computer were to crash while a driver was going 65 miles per hour (105 km/h) down the highway?

Currently, most Americans are generally open to the idea of autonomous vehicles. Fifty-two percent said they would be willing to take a ride in a fully self-driving car, according to a 2015 survey by the World Economic Forum. Yet most parents would not trust an autonomous car enough to let their children ride alone in one. Whereas people have expressed interest in self-driving features like braking, steering, and acceleration, they don't want to give the car total control. This worry might stem from a lack of trust or from a lack of interest in giving up the enjoyment of driving. A 2015 University of Michigan survey found that most respondents—96 percent—would want a steering wheel and gas and brake pedals in their car. The desire for at least partial control wouldn't favor Google's autonomous car model. And, in fact, most consumers say they would feel more comfortable riding in an autonomous car produced by the auto industry

WORDS IN CONTEXT

incremental
Happening in small steps.

Fleets of self-driving cars on the road might inspire fear in some consumers who want more human control over such potentially dangerous machinery. Driverless car companies are doing their best to build trust and confidence in this new technology that they consider very safe.

rather than one made by a computer company like Google.

Manufacturers of self-driving cars are trying to increase consumer trust by building many safeguards into their cars. Audi loaded its A8 model with backup braking and steering systems. If one system fails, the other can take over. And if anything were to go wrong in the software or hardware systems, the car would simply shut down. The technology will need to be almost perfect; if consumers learn about a fatal crash caused by a self-driving car, it could make them too fearful of trying out the technology. Automakers can also build trust by ensuring consumers that their car's computer won't crash or spy on them.

Trust may come a little at a time. Taking small, incremental steps toward driverless cars may help consumers adjust. As consumers try out the technology in bits and pieces—auto park, lane assist, automatic braking—they can begin to judge for themselves whether it works and whether it's worth adopting. "Before the cars of the future can become our pilots, they need to prove themselves as our co-pilots,"[47] writes John Brownlee of *Fast Company* magazine.

What Will the Future Bring?

Self-driving cars are an evolving technology. Whether they take off and how they will ultimately look and drive still remains to be seen. Likewise, it is uncertain whether consumers will embrace cars that drive themselves. Some experts are very cautious about this brave new world of driverless cars. "We need to rethink the notion of progress, not as progress toward full autonomy, but as progress toward trusted, transparent, reliable, safe autonomy that is fully interactive: The car does what I want it to do, and only when I want it to do it," cautions MIT engineering professor David Mindell. He sees a future in which humans don't give full control over driving to their cars. "The notion of ceding control of something as fundamental to life as driving to a big, opaque corporation—people are not comfortable with that."[48]

Others say a world in which cars pilot themselves down highways and back roads is inevitable. "A future without human drivers is a long, long way off," notes Mat Honan, San Francisco bureau chief for the website BuzzFeed. "But we'll get there. No matter what you think. No matter what you hope. No matter how you feel about it. Because the efficient, unemotional, necessary logic of cars that operate without human error and instability is unquestionable."[49]

Source Notes

Introduction: The Driverless Car

1. Alexander Stoklosa, "We Watch an Audi A7 Drive Away and Park in a Garage All by Itself—with No Driver," *Car and Driver* (blog), January 10, 2013. http://blog.caranddriver.com.

Chapter 1: The Earliest Attempts at Self-Driving Cars

2. Norman Bel Geddes, *Magic Motorways.* New York: Random House, 1940.
3. Quoted in Melissa Aparicio, "How We Arrived at Today's Self-Driving Cars—and Where the Road Leads," *PCWorld*, May 14, 2014. www.pcworld.com.
4. John Frank Weaver, *Robots Are People Too: How Siri, Google Car, and Artificial Intelligence Will Force Us to Change Our Laws*. Santa Barbara, CA: Praeger, 2014, p. 53.
5. Quoted in Burkhard Bilger, "Auto Correct," *New Yorker*, November 25, 2013. www.newyorker.com.
6. Quoted in Bilger, "Auto Correct."

Chapter 2: DARPA: Desert and City Challenges

7. Quoted in Marsha Walton, "Robots Fail to Complete Grand Challenge," CNN, May 6, 2004. www.cnn.com.
8. Quoted in Walton, "Robots Fail to Complete Grand Challenge."
9. Quoted in Bilger, "Auto Correct."
10. Quoted in Noah Shachtman, "DARPA Chief Speaks," *Wired*, February 20, 2007. www.wired.com.
11. Quoted in DARPA, "Tartan Racing Wins $2 Million Prize for DARPA Urban Challenge," November 4, 2007. http://archive.darpa.mil.
12. *Popular Mechanics*, "Carnegie Mellon and GM's Boss Wins DARPA Urban Challenge," September 30, 2009. www.popularmechanics.com.

Chapter 3: Developing the First Self-Driving Car

13. TED, "Sebastian Thrun: Google's Driverless Car," March 2011. www.ted.com.
14. Sebastian Thrun, "Leave the Driving to the Car, and Reap Benefits in Safety and Mobility," *New York Times*, December 5, 2011. www.nytimes.com.
15. Quoted in Bilger, "Auto Correct."
16. Quoted in Tom Vanderbilt, "Let the Robot Drive: The Autonomous Car of the Future Is Here," *Wired*, January 20, 2012. www.wired.com.
17. Vanderbilt, "Let the Robot Drive."
18. *Google Official Blog*, "What We're Driving At," October 9, 2010. https://googleblog.blogspot.com.
19. Brandon Griggs, "Google's New Self-Driving Car Has No Steering Wheel or Brake," CNN, May 28, 2014. www.cnn.com.
20. Quoted in Griggs, "Google's New Self-Driving Car Has No Steering Wheel or Brake."
21. Liz Gannes, "A Joy Ride in Google's New Self-Driving Clown Car," Re/code, May 27, 2014. http://recode.net.
22. Quoted in Liz Gannes, "Google's New Self-Driving Car Ditches the Steering Wheel," Re/code, May 27, 2014. http://recode.net/2014/05/27/googles-new-self-driving-car-ditches-the-steering-wheel/.
23. Google, "Google Self-Driving Car Project," June 3, 2015. https://plus.google.com.
24. Bill Howard, "What Is Lane Departure Warning, and How Does It Work?," ExtremeTech, September 3, 2013. www.extremetech.com.
25. Quoted in Molly McHugh, "Tesla's Cars Now Drive Themselves, Kinda," *Wired*, October 14, 2015. www.wired.com.

Chapter 4: Benefits and Barriers to Self-Driving Cars

26. *Consumer Reports*, "Avoiding Crashes with Self-Driving Cars," February 2014. www.consumerreports.org.

27. Quoted in John Markoff, "For Now, Self-Driving Cars Still Need Humans," *New York Times*, January 17, 2016. www.nytimes.com.

28. Quoted in Andrew Del-Colle, "The 12 Most Important Questions About Self-Driving Cars," *Popular Mechanics*, October 8, 2013. www.popularmechanics.com.

29. Jean-Francois Bonnefon, Azim Shariff, and Iyad Rahwan, "Autonomous Vehicles Need Experimental Ethics: Are We Ready for Utilitarian Cars?," Cornell University Library, October 12, 2015. http://arxiv.org.

30. Quoted in Pete Bigelow, "For Self-Driving Cars, Privacy May Be Bigger Concern than Safety," Autoblog, May 12, 2015. www.autoblog.com.

31. Quoted in Markoff, "For Now, Self-Driving Cars Still Need Humans."

32. Megan McArdle, "Self-Driving Cars Will Thrive with More Regulation," Bloomberg View, January 15, 2016. www.bloombergview.com.

33. Quoted in Alex Davies, "Self-Driving Cars Are Legal, but Real Rules Would Be Nice," *Wired*, May 15, 2015. www.wired.com.

34. Quoted in Davies, "Self-Driving Cars Are Legal, but Real Rules Would Be Nice."

35. KPMG, "Automobile Insurance in the Era of Autonomous Vehicles," June 2015. www.kpmg.com.

36. Quoted in Bilger, "Auto Correct."

37. Quoted in Chuck Tannert, "Will You Ever Be Able to Afford a Self-Driving Car?," *Fast Company*, January 31, 2014. www.fastcompany.com.

Chapter 5: Driverless Cars of the Future

38. Quoted in Sami Haj-Assaad, "When Will Self-Driving Cars Really Arrive?," AutoGuide.com, August 11, 2015. www.autoguide.com.

39. Quoted in Bilger, "Auto Correct."

40. Quoted in Sean Keach, "Ford Says Fully Self-Driving Cars on Roads by 2020," Trusted Reviews, January 18, 2016. www.trustedreviews.com.

41. Quoted in Josh Cohen, "Driverless Bus Testing Coming to Bay Area," Next City, October 12, 2015. https://nextcity.org.

42. Quoted in Alex Fitzpatrick, "Why General Motors Is Investing $500 Million in Lyft," *Time*, January 4, 2016. http://time.com.

43. Quoted in Adam Fisher, "Inside Google's Quest to Popularize Self-Driving Cars," *Popular Science,* September 18, 2013. www.popsci.com.

44. AllAmericanCDJ, "2011 Dodge Charger—the Future of Driving—All American Dodge," *YouTube*, April 20, 2011. www.youtube.com.

45. Quoted in McHugh, "Tesla's Cars Now Drive Themselves, Kinda."

46. Quoted in *Consumer Reports*, "Avoiding Crashes with Self-Driving Cars," February 2014. www.consumerreports.org.

47. John Brownlee, "How UI/UX Design Will Map the Future of Self-Driving Cars," *Fast Company,* October 27, 2015. www.fastcodesign.com.

48. Robotics@MIT, "Not So Fast." https://robotics.mit.edu.

49. Mat Honan, "Google's Cute Cars and the Ugly End of Driving," BuzzFeed, September 30, 2015. www.buzzfeed.com.

For Further Research

Books

James E. Duffy, *Modern Automotive Technology*. Tinley Park, IL: Goodheart Wilcox, 2013.

Jane P. Gardner, *Car Science*. Broomall, PA: Mason Crest, 2016.

Levi Tillemann, *The Great Race: The Global Quest for the Car of the Future*. New York: Simon & Schuster, 2015.

S. Van Themsche, *The Advent of Unmanned Electric Vehicles: The Choices Between E-Mobility and Immobility.* Berlin, Germany: Springer, 2015.

John Frank Weaver, *Robots Are People Too: How Siri, Google Car, and Artificial Intelligence Will Force Us to Change Our Laws*. Santa Barbara, CA: Praeger, 2014.

Internet Sources

Burkhard Bilger, "Auto Correct," *New Yorker*, November 25, 2013. www.newyorker.com.

Andrew Del-Colle, "The 12 Most Important Questions About Self-Driving Cars," *Popular Mechanics*, October 8, 2013. www.popularmechanics.com.

Google Official Blog, "What We're Driving At," October 9, 2010. https://googleblog.blogspot.com.

Mat Honan, "Google's Cute Cars and the Ugly End of Driving," BuzzFeed, September 30, 2015. www.buzzfeed.com.

Sebastian Thrun, "Leave the Driving to the Car, and Reap Benefits in Safety and Mobility," *New York Times*, December 5, 2011. www.nytimes.com.

Tom Vanderbilt, "Let the Robot Drive: The Autonomous Car of the Future Is Here," *Wired*, January 20, 2012. www.wired.com.

Websites

Extreme Tech (www.extremetech.com/tag/self-driving-cars). This is a guide to the latest news on self-driving cars.

Google's Self-Driving Car Project (www.google.com/selfdrivingcar/). Google's website gives an overview of its self-driving car project, complete with videos.

Mcity (www.mtc.umich.edu/test-facility). This site offers information on the University of Michigan's Mcity testing facility for autonomous vehicles.

Self-Driving Cars (www.theguardian.com/technology/self-driving-cars). The *Guardian* newspaper's website features an entire section devoted to the latest news about self-driving cars.

Wired (www.wired.com/tag/self-driving-cars/). The online tech publication *Wired* offers its own guide to self-driving cars.

Index

Picture Credits

About the Author

Stephanie Watson is a freelance writer based in Providence, Rhode Island. For nearly two decades she has covered the latest health and science research for publications such as WebMD, Healthline, HowStuffWorks, and Harvard Medical School. Watson has authored more than two dozen books for young adults, including *Brain Injuries in Football* and *Medical Tourism: A Reference Handbook*.